CW01149986

Original title:
Chimes of Winter

Copyright © 2024 Swan Charm
All rights reserved.

Author: Kene Elistrand
ISBN HARDBACK: 978-9908-52-110-7
ISBN PAPERBACK: 978-9908-52-111-4
ISBN EBOOK: 978-9908-52-112-1

Cascades in Crystal Light

In morning's glow, the waters gleam,
A crystal dance, a waking dream.
Soft whispers flow, the breeze is light,
As nature sings in pure delight.

The sunbeams fall on every face,
A tender touch, a warm embrace.
Among the rocks, the shadows play,
While laughter flutters, here to stay.

With every splash, the echoes ring,
The joy it brings, a fleeting fling.
The vibrant hues of blue and green,
In tranquil harmony, serene.

Beneath the pines, by rivers wide,
The gentle currents, they abide.
A symphony of nature's sound,
In crystal waters, peace is found.

As day retreats, the stars ignite,
Cascades whisper in the night.
In dreams, we float on crystal streams,
Forever held in starlit themes.

The Solstice Melody

In twilight hush, the world awakes,
A melody that softly breaks.
The longest day, a sunlit song,
Where fleeting moments all belong.

With every breath, the wildflowers sway,
In colors bright, they greet the day.
The breeze hums low through branches fair,
A whispered tune that fills the air.

As shadows stretch to find their place,
The golden hour, a soft embrace.
Each note of light, pure and divine,
In harmony, the stars align.

The crackling fire, a warm refrain,
As evening weaves its softest chain.
In every heart, a spark ignites,
A solstice dance beneath the lights.

The moon will rise and time will drift,
In silent awe, the night's a gift.
Together sing, let spirits roam,
For in this night, we find our home.

Heartbeats of the Cold

In the stillness, whispers sigh,
Snowflakes dance from a gray sky.
Footprints left, a fleeting trace,
Winter's breath, a soft embrace.

Crystals glimmer on the ground,
Nature's hush, a sacred sound.
Hearts beat slow, in time we find,
A warmth within, though cold outside.

Cascades in Crystal Light

In morning's glow, the waters gleam,
A crystal dance, a waking dream.
Soft whispers flow, the breeze is light,
As nature sings in pure delight.

The sunbeams fall on every face,
A tender touch, a warm embrace.
Among the rocks, the shadows play,
While laughter flutters, here to stay.

With every splash, the echoes ring,
The joy it brings, a fleeting fling.
The vibrant hues of blue and green,
In tranquil harmony, serene.

Beneath the pines, by rivers wide,
The gentle currents, they abide.
A symphony of nature's sound,
In crystal waters, peace is found.

As day retreats, the stars ignite,
Cascades whisper in the night.
In dreams, we float on crystal streams,
Forever held in starlit themes.

Original title:
Chimes of Winter

Copyright © 2024 Swan Charm
All rights reserved.

Author: Kene Elistrand
ISBN HARDBACK: 978-9908-52-110-7
ISBN PAPERBACK: 978-9908-52-111-4
ISBN EBOOK: 978-9908-52-112-1

Echoes from a Winter's Nook

Fires crackle, shadows play,
Crisp air calls the night to stay.
Whispers of wind beneath the eaves,
Nature sleeps, while silence weaves.

Icicles hang from rooftops tall,
A chill wrapped in a frosty shawl.
Memories linger, soft and deep,
In winter's hold, the world does sleep.

Melodies Carried by the Frost

Notes like crystals drift and glide,
Echoed hush where dreams abide.
Silent strings of icy air,
Winter hums a tender prayer.

Lullabies of snow and chill,
Each soft breath, a quiet thrill.
Melodies of the frozen light,
Whisper secrets into the night.

The Frosty Canvas of Night

Stars scatter on a blanket white,
The moon paints dreams in silver light.
A tapestry of cold so vast,
Moments captured, shadows cast.

Breath visible in the frosty air,
Silent wishes float with care.
When night unfolds its chilly art,
The heartbeat of winter stirs the heart.

The Caress of a Frozen Gale

A whisper through the trees,
The chill that bites the skin.
With every breath it frees,
A dance of white begins.

Silver flakes in the air,
Each flutter, light and small.
Branches bow, stripped bare,
In winter's gentle thrall.

Shadows stretch and sway,
As twilight's grace unfolds.
In frost, the dreams at play,
Nature's tale retold.

The night wraps tight its cloak,
Underneath a crescent moon.
In silence, hearts evoke,
A tune of love's sweet boon.

With every gust that sighs,
A story carved in snow.
Beneath the starlit skies,
Frozen gales will flow.

Muffled Melodies in the White

Whispers of the falling flakes,
A serenade throughout.
In snow, the world partakes,
With hush, the silence shouts.

Footsteps soft on the ground,
Each echo holds the night.
In the stillness, they're found,
Wrapped in winter's light.

A hidden song emerges,
From depths of winter's breath.
Melodies like soft surges,
In quietude, there's depth.

The trees wear coats of white,
Their branches bow in tune.
Under the starry sight,
They hum a gentle rune.

In every flake's descent,
A world transformed anew.
With each breath, we are lent,
Muffled joys that ensue.

Glassy Echoes Beneath the Stars

Sparkling lights in the sky,
Reflections on the stream.
A symphony on high,
In the night, we seem.

Ripples dance like whispers,
Underneath the pale glow.
In the dark, time lingers,
As shadows breathe slow.

The glassy surface gleams,
Holding secrets of the past.
In its stillness, it dreams,
Of moments that will last.

Each twinkle tells a tale,
Of love and soft goodbyes.
In the night, we set sail,
Toward endless, bright skies.

Beneath the cosmic gaze,
Where echoes softly play.
In this tranquil phase,
The stars guide the way.

The Softness of Silent Encounters

A glance, a subtle pause,
In the space where time suspends.
With silence as our cause,
Two souls, the night transcends.

With every heartbeat shared,
The air holds magic tight.
In moments long prepared,
We bask in silver light.

The world fades to a hush,
As whispers brush our skin.
With every silent rush,
New beginnings can begin.

In gentle shadows cast,
Where dreams and wishes cling.
We find our symbols vast,
In the hush, our hearts sing.

In stillness, truth unfolds,
In grace, beneath the night.
The softness that it holds,
Encounters pure delight.

Celestial Frost

In silent nights where starlight glows,
The frost descends in shimmering flows.
Each crystal breath holds whispers clear,
Of secrets kept from far and near.

Beneath the moon's soft silver beam,
A world adorned in frosty dream.
Trees wear coats of icy lace,
Nature's calm in frozen grace.

Through misty air, the cold winds sing,
Of winter's touch and stillness bring.
In every flake, a tale is spun,
A dance of ice beneath the sun.

The night unfolds with twinkling eyes,
As shadows weave beneath the skies.
A chill that stirs the heart to pause,
To ponder life and nature's laws.

Twilight's Frosty Muse

As twilight falls with gentle sigh,
A canvas painted in deepening sky.
Frost creeps in on the edges near,
A muse inspired by whispers clear.

The air is crisp, each breath a cloud,
Within the hush, dreams are unbowed.
Soft shadows stretch in lavender hues,
While the world dons its frosty shoes.

In quiet moments, stars awaken,
The twinkling lights in silence shaken.
Twilight's brush begins to wane,
As icy fingers weave the plain.

A symphony of quiet chimes,
Echoes linger through the climes.
Each note a whisper, soft and low,
In frost's embrace, the magic flows.

Twilight Serenade

The twilight skies in colors bloom,
As daylight fades, casting gloom.
A serenade of whispers sweet,
Where shadows dance on frozen street.

The bracing air begins to bite,
As stars emerge, twinkling bright.
A frosty breath upon the morn,
Awakens dreams, where hopes are born.

In dusky corners, secrets hide,
Through shimmering leaves, soft winds glide.
A chorus sung in silver tones,
In every heart, the night enthrones.

Beneath the veil of evening's grace,
The world finds calm in a loving space.
As twilight deepens, spirits rise,
In twilight's serenade, we sigh.

Shimmer of Icy Starlight

When night enfolds in velvet deep,
A shimmer stirs, a world to keep.
Icy starlight dances bright,
Guiding dreams through the chill of night.

The moonlight weaves a silver thread,
Through mountains high and rivers spread.
Each sparkle whispered, soft and clear,
A lullaby for souls to hear.

Frozen whispers in the night,
A tapestry of magical light.
Each flake that falls, a story spun,
Of ancient tales and days long gone.

The shimmer lights the darkened sky,
While shadows linger, soft and shy.
In icy realms where spirits soar,
The starlit echo opens door.

Resonance in the Dark

Whispers echo through the night,
Secrets held in shadows tight.
Stars above begin to gleam,
Hearts entwined within a dream.

Silent footsteps on the ground,
Lost in thoughts, no voice around.
Moonlight casts a silver hue,
Guiding souls in paths anew.

Time stands still in hushed embrace,
Fleeting moments drift with grace.
Breathless sighs and fleeting looks,
Every gaze, a silent book.

Haunting sounds, a distant song,
In the dark, where we belong.
Melodies of love collide,
A universe where shadows hide.

Resonance feels like a spark,
Lighting fires within the dark.
Together, we ignite the night,
Bound by love, a pure delight.

Winter's Breath

Chilling winds cut through the trees,
Whispers carried by the breeze.
Blankets draped in purest white,
Embrace the world in still of night.

Crystal flakes, a soft descent,
Nature's art, a pure content.
Frosted windows, candles glow,
Inside warmth, outside snow.

Frozen branches, twinkling lights,
Silent beauty, starry nights.
Winter's breath caresses slow,
Every flake a gentle show.

Footprints left in fresh, soft snow,
Stories shared in whispers low.
Cups of cocoa, laughter flow,
Memories made as cold winds blow.

Underneath the pale moon's light,
Winter dances, pure and bright.
In its chill, we find our place,
Wrapped in winter's soft embrace.

Dances of the Snowflakes

Spiraling down from skies so high,
Dancing lightly, they drift by.
Each unique in form and grace,
Snowflakes twirl in winter's embrace.

Gentle whispers in the air,
Fleeting moments, soft and rare.
Twilight glows, a dreamlike scene,
Nature's ballet, pure and serene.

They flutter, light as dreams,
Glistening soft in moonlight beams.
Every flake a world untold,
Stories whispered, bright and bold.

Twirling slow in chilly air,
Winter's magic everywhere.
In their dance, time stands still,
Heartbeats echo, frozen thrill.

In the silence, a gentle song,
Melodies where we belong.
Dances of snowflakes bring delight,
Whispers of winter, pure and bright.

Lullabies of the Long Night

Crickets sing a soothing tune,
Underneath the watchful moon.
Gentle shadows, dreams take flight,
Lullabies wrap round the night.

Softly treading, time moves slow,
Whispers in the soft moon's glow.
Every heartbeat a sweet sigh,
Underneath the expansive sky.

Blankets drawn against the chill,
Peace descends as hearts stand still.
Wrapped in warmth, we drift away,
To the songs the night will play.

Melodies of stars above,
Promises and endless love.
Each note falls like silken thread,
Woven dreams in slumber's bed.

In the quiet, hope ignites,
Guiding us through starry nights.
Lullabies, both near and far,
Cradle us beneath the stars.

Lightly Touched by Snow

Silent flakes fall from the sky,
Dancing gently as they fly.
Covering the earth in white,
A soft touch, pure delight.

Branches bow under the weight,
Nature's beauty, a tranquil state.
Footsteps crunch on frozen ground,
Peaceful moments all around.

Children laugh in pure play,
Building dreams on winter's day.
Snowmen rise with carrot noses,
Joy unfurls as winter dozes.

As twilight paints the scene,
Shadows stretch, a serene sheen.
Stars emerge in quiet night,
Whispers of warmth, a gentle light.

Frozen Reverie

The world lies still, hushed in white,
Wrapped in winter's soft, cool light.
Each breath a cloud, each step a dance,
In this frozen, dreamy trance.

Branches cradle frosted dreams,
Glittering in the moon's soft beams.
A quiet lake, a mirrored glow,
A realm where silence starts to flow.

Footprints trace forgotten paths,
Echoes of laughter, distant laughs.
Time stands still, with every breath,
Caught in the beauty of crisp death.

Through the trees, a whisper sighs,
Where the heart of winter lies.
A gentle breeze stirs the air,
Mysteries linger everywhere.

Glistening Dawn

Morning light breaks through the night,
Painting skies with hues so bright.
Dewdrops glisten on the grass,
Nature wakes as moments pass.

Birds chirp softly, greet the morn,
In this world, anew, reborn.
Golden rays kiss every leaf,
Spreading warmth, dispelling grief.

Mountains stand, tall and grand,
Guardians of this enchanted land.
Whispers of the day begin,
A symphony of life within.

As the sun climbs high and near,
All is vibrant, warm, and clear.
In the stillness, dreams take flight,
Glistening dawn, a pure delight.

Whispers in the Air

Softly floating, secrets shared,
Through the trees, the voices bared.
Wrapped in mist, the morning calls,
Nature's stories, heard by all.

Breezes carry tales of old,
In each sigh, the world unfolds.
Listen close, with heart laid bare,
Magic lingers in the air.

Petals dance on fragile stems,
Rays of sun, like golden hems.
Wildflowers sway, a gentle tune,
Painting life beneath the moon.

Every whisper, every sigh,
Echoes softly, passing by.
In the quiet, we will find,
Hearts connected, soul entwined.

A Frosty Waltz of Time

In the stillness, snowflakes dance,
Whispers of winter in a trance.
Moonlight kisses the icy ground,
A waltz of silence, beauty found.

Every breath, a crystal sigh,
As shadows stretch beneath the sky.
Moments freeze in gleaming light,
A soft embrace of frosty night.

Trees adorned in white attire,
Branches glisten, hearts inspire.
Time drifts by on chilly air,
In frozen dreams, the world is rare.

Footprints linger, then dissolve,
In the magic, we resolve.
Winter's song hums sweet and low,
As time waltzes, soft and slow.

Through the frost, we find our way,
A fleeting dance at end of day.
In every flake, a story spun,
A frosty waltz, forever won.

Tranquil Footsteps in the Thaw

As spring whispers to the frost,
A gentle warmth, the chill is lost.
Footsteps echo on the thaw,
Nature's pulse, a sacred law.

The brook awakens from its sleep,
In tender ripples, secrets seep.
Life stirs slowly, green appears,
Washing away the winter's tears.

Petals open, colors bloom,
Underneath the sun's soft loom.
Every bud a hopeful sign,
In tranquil steps, we intertwine.

Birdsongs fill the morning air,
A symphony beyond compare.
In every note, a tale unfolds,
Of tranquil joys that spring beholds.

As paths unwind in golden rays,
We'll walk together through the days.
In the heart of nature's grace,
We'll find our peace in this embrace.

Silent Affections of the Frost

Beneath the veil of winter's breath,
Lies a love that conquers death.
Silent whispers in the night,
Affection blooms in cold twilight.

Frosted windows tell our tale,
Of tender hearts that never fail.
In every flake, a memory lies,
A silent promise that never dies.

Underneath the starry dome,
Warmth arises, finding home.
Two souls dance on frozen ground,
In silent rhythms, joy is found.

As twilight fades into the day,
Love's quiet glow will light the way.
With every heartbeat, spirits soar,
Silent affections, forevermore.

Through the chill, we learn to see,
The warmth in sweet simplicity.
In winter's grasp, our hearts ignite,
Together in this frosty night.

Ethereal Echoes in the Chill

In the world where silence reigns,
Ethereal echoes, soft refrains.
The air is thick with whispered tales,
As winter breathes, and beauty pales.

Snowflakes drift like feathered dreams,
Catching light in silver beams.
Each echo carries warmth within,
An invitation, a quiet spin.

In the chill, time stretches wide,
Mysteries bloom where shadows hide.
Nature's canvas, painted white,
In ethereal glow, we take flight.

Frosted branches sway and bend,
With each whisper, heartaches mend.
In the cold, we find the grace,
Of winter's touch, a soft embrace.

As the chill wraps snug and tight,
We gather close through starry night.
In echoes soft, we feel the thrill,
Of love's warmth in winter's chill.

Echoes in the Quietude

In a hush where shadows play,
Whispers dance, then fade away.
Stars above begin to gleam,
Lost within a silent dream.

Softly stirring, breaths collide,
Moonlit paths where secrets hide.
Time stands still, a fleeting glance,
Caught within this shadowed trance.

Echoes linger, heartbeats slow,
In the stillness, spirits flow.
Gentle winds through trees they weave,
Nature sighs, and we believe.

Each moment carries, weightless sigh,
Silent songs that never die.
In this realm where night descends,
Echoes of the past, our friends.

Awake in dreams, we softly tread,
Through the quiet, softly led.
Embraced by peace, we find our place,
In the echoes, time we trace.

Silver Notes in the Depths of Blue

In the ocean's gentle sway,
Silver fish in light play.
Beneath waves, a world unfolds,
Stories whispered, truths retold.

Deep in azure, shadows gleam,
Liquid lullabies, a dream.
Coral gardens sway with grace,
Nature's heart in a sacred space.

Songs of currents flow and weave,
In the depths, we learn to believe.
Melodies born from the tide,
Silver notes like stars collide.

Echoes linger in the sea,
Tales of time and mystery.
Where the sunlight cannot reach,
Richest wisdom, the waves teach.

As the tides of life will roll,
Each note plays upon the soul.
In the depths of blue we find,
Harmony for heart and mind.

Chilled Ballads of the Hearth

In the glow of embers bright,
Stories shared on winter nights.
Whispers warm in shadows cast,
Moments gathered, hearts amassed.

Wrapped in blankets, cozy glow,
Outside, fleeting flakes of snow.
Each soft flurry, quiet song,
In the hearth, where we belong.

Voices rise like sweet perfume,
Warming up the chilly room.
Hand in hand, in laughter play,
Chilled ballads melt away grey.

Time suspends as memories soar,
Every tale opens a door.
In the crackle, love ignites,
Filling up those starry nights.

Through the warmth, connections deepen,
In this space, our spirits leaven.
Chilled ballads, songs we share,
Within the hearth, love finds its care.

Secrets in the Snowfall

Softly falling, crystals light,
Cloth of white embraces night.
Whispers carried on the breeze,
Secrets wrapped in winter's tease.

Pine trees hush beneath the weight,
Stories bound in frozen fate.
Footsteps muffled, silence reigns,
Magic cloaked in snowy veils.

With each flake, a new embrace,
Nature sings in endless grace.
In the stillness, hearts align,
Secrets shared, our spirits twine.

As the world wears purest white,
Dreams take flight in winter's light.
Underneath these blanket skies,
Hidden truths and soft goodbyes.

Each snowfall whispers, memories hold,
In the chill, love dare be bold.
Wrapped in warmth, we sit and gaze,
At the secrets winter lays.

Winter's Whispered Thoughts

Snowflakes dance in the air,
Silent wishes softly shared.
The world is wrapped in pure white,
Dreams echo through the night.

Cold winds weave through bare trees,
Whispers carried on the breeze.
The moon glows with silver light,
Guiding lost souls in their flight.

Footprints fade on snowy ground,
In this stillness, peace is found.
Stars twinkle, a frosty gleam,
Awakening the winter dream.

Nature holds its gentle breath,
Cradled in the hush of death.
Yet life sleeps beneath the snow,
Awaiting spring's warm, tender glow.

In this quiet, hearts can mend,
Winter's magic, friend to friend.
Embrace the chill, let it flow,
In whispered thoughts, love will grow.

Hearts Wrapped in Cold

Frost upon the window pane,
A chilly touch, a soft refrain.
Hearts wrapped tight in scarves of wool,
Longing for warmth, love to pull.

Candles flicker, shadows play,
Inside we gather, night and day.
Chilled hands clasped, a gentle squeeze,
Finding refuge, heart's reprise.

Icicles hang like frozen tears,
Each drop carries our hidden fears.
Yet close together, warmth ignites,
Fading the sharpness of cold nights.

Laughter echoes in the room,
Fading all our winter gloom.
Hot cocoa in a stolen glance,
Love wrapped in this wintry dance.

As we face the chilly air,
Know that warmth is always there.
Hearts entwined, we'll brave the frost,
For in this love, we count no cost.

Breath of the Frozen Branches

Branches lace against the sky,
Etched in ice, the world complies.
Nature whispers, soft and low,
In her breath, the secrets flow.

Moonlight scatters on the ground,
Echoes of a winsome sound.
Frosted boughs, a silent choir,
Singing soft of love and fire.

A world wrapped in crystal dreams,
Frigid air, the bright sun gleams.
Every branch tells a story,
Of winter's hush and ancient glory.

Creatures pause in cold surprise,
Finding warmth in each other's eyes.
In the silence, life's embrace,
A tender touch, a soft trace.

When the freeze begins to thaw,
New life stirs, begins to draw.
Yet in this winter's tender clutch,
We find love's breath, a gentle touch.

Sounds of a Still Evening

The dusk settles, soft and deep,
Wrapped in silence, the world sleeps.
Soft whispers in the fading light,
Embracing shadows of the night.

Crickets chirp, a lonesome tune,
Underneath the watchful moon.
Each rustle stirs the tranquil air,
Nature's speech, profound and rare.

Snow crunches beneath weary feet,
Echoes of a day's retreat.
The world awaits, so hushed, so still,
With every breath, the night, we fill.

Stars awaken, one by one,
Threads of silver, dusk undone.
In this stillness, hearts unite,
Bound by whispers of the night.

As the evening softly flows,
Calmness in the winter glows.
Lost in sounds that softly weave,
In this still, we learn to believe.

Shimmering Secrets

In the twilight's gentle glow,
Whispers dance, secrets flow.
Stars twinkle, dreams take flight,
Wrapped in the heart of night.

Moonlit paths lead away,
Through the woods where shadows play.
Every leaf holds a tale,
Nature's magic in the veil.

Breezes hum a soft refrain,
Carrying the echo of rain.
Hidden glades, a sacred keep,
Where time slows and spirits leap.

Glistening dew on petals bright,
Sparkling gems in morning light.
Each moment, a treasure found,
Shimmering secrets all around.

In the silence, hearts draw near,
In whispered dreams, we steer.
Together, in this dance we wade,
In shimmering light, our fears evade.

Notes on a Winter's Breath

The world wrapped in a silver guise,
As snowflakes fall from cloudy skies.
Each breath hangs like frozen glass,
Whispers of winter as moments pass.

Frosted trees stand tall and still,
Silent sentinels on the hill.
The air is crisp, the silence deep,
In winter's embrace, we gently sleep.

Footprints trace the paths we roam,
In this cold, we find a home.
Hushed tones fill the evening air,
A tranquil peace, beyond compare.

The hearth's warmth calls us near,
In cozy corners, we persevere.
With mugs of cocoa, laughter spills,
As winter's chill our hearts fulfills.

A quilt of stars adorns the night,
Shimmering softly, pure and bright.
In the stillness, dreams take wing,
Notes on winter's breath we sing.

Softly Falling

Petals drift from cherry trees,
Carried gently on the breeze.
Softly falling like a sigh,
Nature's whisper, a lullaby.

In the hush of morning light,
Colors blush in pure delight.
Every hue, a story told,
In each petal, love unfolds.

Drifting clouds in skies of blue,
Casting shadows, old and new.
Life unfolds in every glance,
In nature's grace, we find our dance.

With every heartbeat, time stands still,
In these moments, hearts we fill.
Softly falling, memories blend,
Creating paths that never end.

Through gardens rich, we find our way,
In tender blooms, hopes will stay.
Comfort found in a world so bright,
Softly falling, pure delight.

Trills Beneath the Snow

Winter blankets the world in white,
Yet life stirs beneath, out of sight.
Whispers dance on icy air,
As melodies weave through the cold, rare.

Beneath the frost, a heart beats strong,
In quietude, it hums a song.
Trills emerge from hidden nooks,
In harmony with frozen brooks.

Icicles hang like crystal chimes,
Telling tales of warmer climes.
The chill may grip, the wind may blow,
But hope sings sweetly, beneath the snow.

As daylight fades, shadows grow long,
Each moment wrapped in nature's song.
The quiet still, a gentle call,
Trills beneath the snow for all.

With spring's promise not far away,
The whispers grow bolder every day.
In nature's time, the world will flow,
Life will rise, from beneath the snow.

Echoes of Frosted Whispers

Whispers in the frosted air,
Gentle sighs of winter's care.
Silent shadows dance and play,
Echoes of the ending day.

Moonlight glistens on the trees,
Carried softly by the breeze.
Footsteps crunch on frozen ground,
Nature's voice, a haunting sound.

Frosted petals, crisp and bright,
Glistening in the pale moonlight.
Every breath a cloud of white,
Moments frozen, pure delight.

Stars above in velvet skies,
Whisper secrets, soothing sighs.
Nature wraps her arms around,
In her peace, we are unbound.

Time stands still, the world at rest,
In this hush, we feel the blessed.
Echoes linger, sweet and pure,
Frosted whispers that endure.

Bells Beneath the Snow

Bells are ringing, sounds so clear,
Underneath the soft white sphere.
Notes that dance on chilly air,
Caroling your childhood care.

Crisp and bright, the world aglow,
As if painted in fallen snow.
Muffled laughter fills the night,
Wrapped in warmth, our hearts take flight.

Frosty branches, silver white,
Glisten softly in the light.
Each sweet chime a memory,
Carried forth from you to me.

Candles flicker, shadows play,
As the night slips slowly away.
Bells beneath the heavy snow,
We sing loud, our joy to show.

In this season's gentle hold,
Wonders bloom as tales unfold.
Bells are ringing through the dark,
Lighting up our spirit's spark.

Serenade of Silent Nights

In the calm of silent nights,
Nature hums in soft delights.
Stars alight in shimmering grace,
As the moon begins to trace.

Whispers swirl like falling snow,
Every flake a tale to sow.
Dreamers drift on clouds of peace,
In the night, our worries cease.

Crickets sing a lullaby,
Underneath the darkened sky.
Rustling leaves, a sweet refrain,
Nature's chorus, soft as rain.

Shadows linger, softly creep,
While the world drifts off to sleep.
Serenade of tranquil dreams,
Woven through the starlit seams.

Holding tightly to this night,
Where the heart feels pure delight.
Silent whispers everywhere,
In each moment, love and care.

Cold Breath of Dawn

With a shiver, morning breaks,
Cold breath stirs the silent lakes.
Sky reflects a pale blue hue,
As the world begins anew.

Frosty air ignites the chill,
Whispers echo, soft and still.
Birdsongs pierce the morning veil,
Carrying a sweet, warm tale.

Golden rays peak through the trees,
Stirring life with gentle ease.
Nature wakes, begins to glow,
Dewdrops shine like pearls in tow.

Every leaf and blade of grass,
Catches light as moments pass.
Cold breath dances on our skin,
A reminder to begin.

As the sun ascends the sky,
All the shadows fade and die.
With each dawn, a chance to see,
Life's sweet song, our harmony.

Stillness Wrapped in Glass

In a world where silence breathes,
Time stands still, nature weaves.
Reflections dance, shadows play,
Moments caught, they softly sway.

Each glimmer holds a tale untold,
Whispers of warmth in the bitter cold.
Fragile thoughts like drifting snow,
Behind the glass, they ebb and flow.

Life encased, a fleeting glance,
Every shimmer sparks a chance.
Caught in stillness, hearts align,
Wrapped in glass, our souls entwine.

Echoes linger with the light,
Shades of beauty, pure and bright.
Moments frozen, yet they move,
In stillness, we find our groove.

Time's embrace, a breath so sweet,
In the quiet, life feels complete.
Wrapped in dreams, aglow in grace,
In this stillness, we find our place.

Whispered Hues of Twilight

In twilight's soft and fading glow,
Colors blend, a gentle flow.
Whispers linger in the air,
Secrets shared, beyond compare.

The sky adorned with hints of gold,
Stories of the day retold.
Pastel shades begin to blend,
Painting shadows without end.

Nature sighs, the world at rest,
Stillness wrapped in twilight's quest.
Every hue, a soothing balm,
Whispered dreams, enchanting calm.

In the dusk, the stars awake,
Promises made, no hearts will break.
Colors whisper, night unfolds,
In twilight's arms, life gently holds.

Each fleeting moment, oh so sweet,
In whispered hues, our spirits meet.
Embraced by night, we softly drift,
In twilight's glow, our souls uplift.

Twilight's Icy Reverie

As daylight fades, the chill descends,
In twilight's arms, the silence bends.
Shadows dance on frozen ground,
A reverie where peace is found.

The air is crisp, a breath of frost,
With every moment, never lost.
Whispers float like drifting snow,
In icy realms where dreams can grow.

Time slows down; the heart takes flight,
In twilight's grasp, we find the light.
Reflections shimmer, soft and clear,
Amidst the stillness, we draw near.

Beneath the stars, a world unfolds,
Wrapped in magic, stories told.
The icy hues bring solace sweet,
In twilight's dream, our hearts can meet.

With every breath, we feel the grace,
In twilight's arms, we find our place.
A reverie, divine and rare,
In icy whispers, love is bare.

Frosty Fingerprints on Glass

A breath upon the window clear,
Frosty patterns whisper near.
Nature's art, a fleeting trace,
Fingerprints, a soft embrace.

In icy blooms, the world ignites,
Cold designs in starry nights.
Every swirl tells tales of time,
A frosty dance, a silent rhyme.

Shimmers gleam like dreams reborn,
In the cold, our hearts are worn.
A moment held, forever cast,
In glassy whispers, shadows last.

Beneath the frost, memories flow,
In every groove, love stirs below.
Frosty echoes of days gone by,
On frozen glass, we wonder why.

Yet through the chill, a warmth resides,
In every breath where love abides.
Frosty fingerprints, a cherished mark,
In glass, we find the spark.

A Poetic Chill

In winter's clutch, the world stands still,
With breath of frost, the air does chill.
Each flake a whisper, dance in flight,
The moon hangs low, a silver light.

Trees frosted white, dressed in lace,
A quiet beauty, a frozen space.
Footprints trace where shadows wane,
In this serene embrace, no pain.

The winds do sing a haunting song,
A lonesome tune that lasts so long.
Beneath the stars, in calm repose,
Nature's secrets, softly doze.

A world in white, a perfect dream,
Reflecting hopes like a still stream.
In icy grasp, the heart finds peace,
A moment's pause, the chaos cease.

Yet deeper still, the night descends,
A hush that wraps and softly bends.
In every breath, a tale retold,
Of warmth concealed in winter's cold.

Serenities of Shimmering Ice

Glistening crystals in the dawn,
Every ray a magic spawned.
Nature's canvas, so pristine,
Reflecting life in shades of green.

The frozen paths invite the heart,
Where dreams and reality depart.
Embraced by winter's gentle hand,
A realm of peace, a calming land.

Soft whispers echo through the trees,
Filling the air with subtle ease.
A tranquil hush blankets the earth,
In every pause, the sound of mirth.

Amidst the ice, the brook does hum,
A symphony of nature's drum.
In shimmering light, the soul takes flight,
Finding warmth in the coldest night.

With every step, the heart does sway,
In shimmering ice, we find our way.
Nature's artistry on full display,
In this serene and frosty ballet.

Echoing Footfalls Through the Cold

With every step upon the ground,
An echo soft, a whispered sound.
Footfalls mark the winter's reign,
On snowflakes bright, we dance again.

The silence stretches, deep and vast,
Each moment held, the present cast.
Where shadows linger, soft and low,
Through swirling flakes, the cold winds blow.

Crimson cheeks and laughter soar,
In this embrace, we thirst for more.
Together on this frozen trail,
Our spirits rise, we shall not fail.

The world transforms to white and blue,
Each breath of ice, a kiss anew.
In every crunch beneath our feet,
A melody of winter's beat.

As twilight dims, the stars ignite,
In cold embrace, the heart feels light.
We weave through dark, where dreams take form,
Echoing footfalls, we ride the storm.

Nature's Silent Hymn

Amongst the trees, a stillness falls,
A quiet hymn, nature calls.
With every gust, the branches sway,
In harmony, they find their way.

The snowflakes dance, a gentle grace,
Each one unique, none out of place.
A chorus sung by the winter's breath,
In every flake, a promise of rest.

The world adorned in sparkling white,
Under the watch of the silver night.
A tranquil scene, where time does bend,
In nature's arms, we find a friend.

With every pause, the heart beats slow,
In this vast quiet, wonder flows.
The trees stand tall, the mountains loom,
In nature's silent, sweet perfume.

In every moment, peace aligns,
With whispers soft, the world defines.
A symphony composed by wind and earth,
A gentle reminder of what love is worth.

Whirling Winds and Frosted Air

In the night sky, the stars gleam bright,
Whirls of wind dance with delight.
Frosted breath hangs in the night air,
Beneath a blanket of silver flare.

Silent whispers of nature's tune,
Sweeping shadows 'neath the moon.
Branches creak in a gentle sway,
As winter claims the fading day.

Dust of snowflakes falls so light,
Painting the world in colors white.
The chill wraps close, a tender hug,
Where warmth resides, snug as a bug.

Glimmers of ice on every tree,
Nature's art, wild and free.
The whirling winds join the fray,
Guiding dreams on a frosty ballet.

Cloaked in Winter's Gentle Song

The world adorned in white so pure,
Softly sings, the heart's allure.
A cloak of snow on silent ground,
Where peace and joy are truly found.

Footsteps crunch on frosty trails,
As winter whispers with soothing gales.
Each moment wrapped in chilly grace,
In winter's warmth, we find our place.

Branches bow with icy weight,
Radiating a quiet fate.
The dawn breaks with a pastel glow,
Inviting dreams like the falling snow.

Cascades of white through tender trees,
Breathe in magic on the breeze.
Cloaked in winter's gentle song,
Together here, we all belong.

The Frost's Soft Embrace

Whispers of frost upon the grass,
In morning's light, shimmering pass.
A world transformed by winter's kiss,
In the stillness, we find our bliss.

Air crisp and clear, each breath a gift,
Nature's beauty, a gentle lift.
The frost's embrace, so cool and light,
Wraps the day, serene and bright.

Soft blankets of white lie in wait,
As hearts unfold, welcoming fate.
With every flake, a story told,
In nature's arms, we feel consoled.

The calm surrounds, a soothing sound,
In the frosty chill, peace is found.
Embraced by winter, we remain,
In the warmth of love, free from pain.

Icy Sketches of Serenity

Frozen rivers glide with grace,
Mirrored skies in a tranquil space.
Icy sketches on each pane,
Nature's artwork, a sweet refrain.

Crystal patterns twirl and flow,
As time dances soft and slow.
Each snowy peak, a mountain proud,
Whispering secrets, wrapped in shroud.

Branches laced in shimmering white,
Under stars that twinkle bright.
Serenity finds us in this cold,
In the arms of winter, we unfold.

The echoes linger, soft and dear,
In icy realms, we shed our fear.
Wrapped in stillness, dreams will soar,
Icy sketches beckon for more.

Songs of the Longest Night

In shadows deep, the whispers play,
Where stars above begin to sway.
The moonlight sings a gentle tune,
As dreams emerge beneath the rune.

Soft breaths of wind through trees do glide,
While time stands still, a turning tide.
The night unfolds her velvet arms,
Embracing us with hidden charms.

A tapestry of shadows spun,
Emotions dance, each thread begun.
The universe, so vast, so wide,
Keeps secrets locked, where hearts confide.

In starlit dreams, we find our peace,
Through darkest hours, our worries cease.
With every heartbeat, we ignite,
The songs resound in longest night.

So linger here, beneath the sky,
Our spirits sparkle, soaring high.
In unity, we find our light,
Together bound, through longest night.

Frosted Symphony

Upon the ground, the crystals gleam,
A world awash in winter's dream.
The air is crisp, a sweet embrace,
The frosted branches hold their grace.

A symphony of silence plays,
As snowflakes whirl in gentle ways.
The echoes of a season near,
Resound through woods that we hold dear.

In stillness, every heartbeat stands,
While nature weaves with silver hands.
Each flake a note, a whispered sound,
Creating music all around.

The twilight paints the world in white,
As winter weaves her cloak of night.
In harmony, the cold wind sighs,
A frosted symphony that flies.

As stars emerge in skies so bold,
We gather warmth against the cold.
In every breath, a tale unfolds,
Of winter's heart and secrets told.

Lullabies of the Frozen Moon

Beneath the glow of silver light,
The frozen moon, so pure and bright.
It hums a tune, a soft refrain,
Lulling the world to sleep again.

With every shimmer, dreams take flight,
As shadows dance in quiet night.
The branches sway, the nightbirds sing,
A magic woven in the spring.

The stars align in cosmic grace,
Reflecting love on nature's face.
The frosty air, a gentle balm,
In lullabies, the heart feels calm.

We wrap our souls in warmth of night,
Embracing dreams until the light.
The frozen moon, our guide and muse,
In whispered tones, we cannot lose.

So close your eyes, embrace the sound,
In every heartbeat, warmth is found.
For lullabies of night will weave,
A tapestry of dreams to believe.

Glistening Echoes

From valleys deep, the echoes rise,
With glistening light that fills the skies.
They dance upon the winds that roam,
A call to hearts, to find their home.

Each whispered note is soft and clear,
Reminding us that love is near.
Through scattered leaves, the echoes play,
Awakening the dreams of day.

With every sound, a story shared,
Of moments lost, of hearts that dared.
The glistening hues of twilight fade,
Yet in our hearts, the hues cascade.

So linger here, where echoes blend,
Beside the trails where spirits mend.
In glistening charms, we come alive,
Together, we will always thrive.

The stars above bear witness true,
As glistening echoes whisper through.
With every breath, our spirits soar,
In unity, forevermore.

Frosted Midnight

The moonlight drapes the world in white,
A cloak of frost, a veil so bright.
Stars twinkle in the chilly air,
Whispers float without a care.

Trees stand tall, adorned in frost,
Their silent beauty, never lost.
In this serene and frozen night,
Dreams take flight in soft moonlight.

Shapes of shadows dance and play,
In the stillness, they drift away.
Each breath puffs like clouds of mist,
In this moment, nothing's missed.

Winter's hush, a gentle song,
Holds the heart, where it belongs.
In frozen whispers, secrets weave,
A frosted midnight, we believe.

Yet dawn will break with warming light,
Melting dreams of the cold night.
But in our hearts, this night will stay,
Frosted memories won't decay.

Note of the Quiet Woods

Among the trees, a stillness reigns,
Where silence swells, the heart maintains.
Footfalls faint on earthy ground,
In nature's arms, peace is found.

Sunlight filters, dappling green,
A timeless beauty, softly seen.
Whispers of winds brush through the leaves,
A melody only the forest believes.

Birds call out, a gentle tune,
Filling the space, a sweet monsoon.
Nature sings in perfect harmony,
An ode to life, wild and free.

Mossy carpets cushion each step,
In this embrace, worries are swept.
The quiet surrounds, a blanket warm,
Wrapped in comfort, safe from harm.

Here, a moment feels like years,
The soul finds ease, the mind clears.
A simple note, yet so profound,
In the quiet woods, bliss is found.

Serenity in Silver Veils

Morning breaks with silver light,
Veiling dreams from the night.
Mist dances on the water's skin,
A quiet peace, the day begins.

Flowers bloom in muted hues,
Dewdrops glisten like morning views.
Nature stirs in gentle grace,
In this beauty, we find our place.

Birds awaken, a soft refrain,
Songs that wash away the pain.
In the chorus of the dawn,
All our troubles seem withdrawn.

Each breath a whisper, calm and slow,
In silver veils, our spirits flow.
The world unfolds with tender hands,
Where every heartbeat understands.

A haven found between the trees,
A silent hug, a gentle breeze.
In moments shared, our worries pale,
In serenity, we set sail.

The Thawing Silence

Winter's grip begins to fade,
Nature's beauty, softly laid.
Rivers sing as ice breaks free,
A symphony of jubilee.

Whispers linger in the thaw,
Awakening the earth's great awe.
Buds peek through the melting snow,
A promise of life, a gentle glow.

The air is sweet with hints of spring,
Each day unfurls, a wondrous thing.
Birds return, a joyful choir,
Spreading hope like wildfire.

Sunlight kisses the warming ground,
In this transition, joy is found.
Beauty rises, bright and bold,
In the thawing silence, stories told.

Emerging life, a vibrant scene,
In every corner, shades of green.
Nature dances, a lively spree,
In the thawing silence, we are free.

Muffled Footsteps in Snow

Footprints vanish in the white,
Each step echoes, soft and light.
A world wrapped in silence, pure,
Nature's calm, a winter cure.

Swaying branches, gently bend,
Whispers in the cold ascend.
Soft flakes fall, a dance so slow,
Veiling earth in tranquil glow.

Each breath steams in frosty air,
Winter's magic everywhere.
The heart beats to a silent drum,
As time slips by, a feeling numb.

Night descends, the sky a show,
Stars emerge, a softened glow.
In this landscape, dreams unfold,
A tapestry of stories told.

Muffled footsteps tread with care,
In this stillness, secrets share.
A journey through the endless white,
Guided softly by the night.

Luminous Shadows

In the twilight's fading kiss,
Shadows dance, an ethereal bliss.
Flickering lights, a gentle glow,
Whispers of magic in the flow.

Underneath the fading sky,
Dreams awaken, spirits fly.
Luminous whispers softly fall,
In this realm, we hear the call.

The night holds stories yet untold,
Figures move, both brave and bold.
Dancing softly, they entwine,
In the dark, their bodies shine.

Colors blend in twilight's art,
Each shadow plays a vital part.
A symphony of night begun,
Guided by the silver sun.

Luminous shadows cast their spell,
In the quiet, where secrets dwell.
Each flicker tells a tale divine,
In this hush, the stars align.

Winter's Gentle Song

A lullaby of falling snow,
Whispers of winter, soft and slow.
Trees don coats of sparkling white,
Nature's hymn, a pure delight.

The brook sings beneath a frost,
In its music, warmth is lost.
Yet still it flows, a gentle hand,
Guiding us through this silent land.

Snowflakes twirl on whispered breeze,
Carrying tales from distant trees.
Dancing flakes, a soft embrace,
In this stillness, find your space.

The twilight glows with silver hue,
A canvas painted fresh and new.
Every corner, every nook,
Awakens dreams, like an open book.

Winter's song, a tranquil call,
Uniting hearts, embracing all.
In this moment, pause and breathe,
As nature wraps us in her weave.

Tranquil Frost

Morning light breaks through the mist,
Frosty air, a chilly kiss.
Nature's palate, crisp and bright,
Wraps the world in pure delight.

Crunching leaves beneath my feet,
Echoes of a winter beat.
Each breath clouding, soft and clear,
In this moment, all is near.

Sunrise paints the pines aglow,
Silver branches, soft and slow.
Delicate crystals, nature's art,
Every glimmer plays its part.

Stillness blankets all around,
In the silence, peace is found.
Frosty patterns grace the ground,
Where only whispers can be found.

Tranquil frost, a gentle friend,
As the day begins to blend.
In every shadow, every light,
Winter's touch, a pure delight.

The Veil of Frosted Conversations

Whispers dance on icy air,
Words like snowflakes, light and rare.
Each breath a ghost, a fleeting trace,
Beneath the veil, we share this space.

Frozen thoughts in twilight glow,
Fractured tales from long ago.
In silence, dreams begin to weave,
This fragile moment we believe.

Echoes shiver, hearts entwine,
Frosted secrets, yours and mine.
As shadows stretch and daylight fades,
We linger here, where hope invades.

Time slips by like winter's chill,
Yet warmth ignites, a quiet thrill.
Through icy ties, our spirits rise,
In frosted whispers, truth never lies.

So let this moment softly rest,
In peace, we wear our quiet vest.
Beneath the veil, we find our grace,
In frosted conversations, we embrace.

Silence Woven in White

Blanketed dreams in silence lie,
Woven whispers beneath the sky.
Soft footsteps tread on snow-draped ground,
Here in stillness, peace is found.

Frosted trees stand tall and bare,
Silent stories fill the air.
Each flake a thread, a tale untold,
In this quiet, hearts grow bold.

Moonlight glimmers on icy streams,
Reflecting all our wistful dreams.
In the hush, we find our place,
Wrapped in warmth, in winter's grace.

Stars above in velvet night,
Guiding lost souls with gentle light.
Each moment flows like drifting snow,
In silence, love begins to grow.

Together bathed in silver hue,
Every glance speaks, pure and true.
In this woven world of white,
We cherish all that feels so right.

Night's Winter Kiss

The night descends, a velvet shroud,
Breathless whispers, soft and proud.
A kiss of frost on tender skin,
The chilly charm makes the heart spin.

Stars awaken in the frozen haze,
Illuminating a dreamy maze.
Shadows linger, secrets shared,
Two souls entwined, all fears laid bare.

In the quiet, time stands still,
Magic rises, a gentle thrill.
With every breath, the world slows down,
As winter's kiss claims the town.

Underneath this blanket of night,
The moon smiles, casting silver light.
In laughter, joy begins to spark,
Echoing softly through the dark.

Together we find warmth anew,
In this embrace, just me and you.
Night's winter kiss, forever bright,
A tender bond in the still of night.

The Lingering Fragrance of Cold

A scent of frost hangs in the air,
Cool whispers brush against my hair.
Each breath a hint of winter's glow,
Telling tales of seasons slow.

The crispness lingers, sharp and bright,
Filling hearts with joyous light.
Snowflakes dance, their story told,
In every flake, a dream enfold.

Chill winds carry memories near,
Of laughter shared, with friends so dear.
In the silence, echoes chime,
The fragrance of cold, a soft rhyme.

As fires crackle and embers gleam,
We gather close, lost in a dream.
With every scent, we reminisce,
In the cold, we find our bliss.

So let the winter's breath linger on,
In the fragrance of morning dawn.
We'll hold this chill with hearts so bold,
In the magic of stories told.

Shimmering Shadows in the Gloom

In the quiet night, whispers low,
Figures dance where soft winds blow.
Moonlight casts its gentle grace,
Shadows flicker, lose their place.

Amidst the dark, a flicker bright,
Illuminates the fragile light.
Beneath the stars, secrets sigh,
Echoes linger, then pass by.

Veils of mystery softly weave,
In the stillness, hearts believe.
Shimmering dreams on the horizon,
Hope ignites with every sigh.

Silhouettes in twilight's embrace,
Dreamers lost in time and space.
With every heartbeat, shadows rise,
In the gloom, life never dies.

As dawn approaches, shadows wane,
Yet in our souls, they still remain.
Embers glow where light will peek,
Shimmering shadows, bright yet meek.

Frosted Rhythms of Dusk

As daylight fades, the chill sets in,
A symphony where night begins.
Trees adorned with icy lace,
Nature's beauty, time's embrace.

Footfalls crunch on frosty ground,
Where silence whispers all around.
Breath like smoke in winter's air,
Moments captured, pure and rare.

Stars awaken, twinkling bright,
Guiding travelers through the night.
The moon hangs low, a silver coin,
Casting dreams where hearts conjoin.

Every rustle, soft and low,
Tells the tales of days long ago.
Frosted rhythms softly play,
Harmonies of dusk's ballet.

In shadows deep, our hopes take flight,
Dancing softly into the night.
With every breath, we find our way,
In this winter's lullaby's sway.

A Tapestry of Stillness

In the quiet, time stands still,
Gentle breezes blend with thrill.
Threads of silence weave and fold,
Stories whispered, yet untold.

Luminous dawn breaks with grace,
Illuminates the tranquil space.
Colors blend, a painter's dream,
Where stillness flows like a stream.

Every heartbeat softly sings,
In the calm, the spirit clings.
Nature's breath, a lullaby,
In stillness lost, we learn to fly.

Moments linger, time unwinds,
Within the stillness, peace we find.
A tapestry of dreams unfold,
In quiet hues of blue and gold.

Here in stillness, we belong,
A world wrapped in the sweetest song.
In every pause, a life anew,
A tapestry in every view.

Glacial Currents of Sound

In the distance, a soft refrain,
Whispers echo, sweet as rain.
Glacial currents flow with ease,
Carrying secrets through the trees.

Beneath the ice, the world resounds,
Every heartbeat, nature's bounds.
Songs of ages, slowly glide,
Melodies that never hide.

The cracking ice, a symphony,
Resonates with destiny.
Voices rise from cold embrace,
An ancient echo finds its place.

Frosted notes in the air will dance,
Each sound inviting, a sacred chance.
In the stillness, harmony found,
Within the glacial currents of sound.

As winter wanes, the notes remain,
A ballet etched in frost and rain.
With every change, the music swells,
Tales of land that nature tells.

Echoing Footfalls

In shadowed halls where whispers tread,
The echoes linger, softly spread.
Each footfall tells a tale untold,
Of secrets buried, brave and bold.

Through corridors of time we roam,
In search of solace, seeking home.
The past resounds with every step,
A haunting rhythm, words unsaid.

The wooden floors, they creak and sigh,
As memories dance, they rise and fly.
A spectral waltz in curtained night,
With each return, the heart takes flight.

Beneath the gaze of silvered moons,
The air alive with ancient tunes.
Among the shadows, dreams unfold,
In echo's arms, new stories mold.

Yet silence weaves its sacred thread,
In quiet moments, hopes are bred.
Through echoing footfalls, we press on,
Towards dawn's embrace, the dark is gone.

Ethereal Hush

In twilight's glow, the stars awake,
While gentle winds begin to shake.
A tranquil hush wraps 'round the night,
As dreams descend, soft and light.

The moonbeams touch the silent ground,
In every corner, peace is found.
The world sighs deep, the thoughts align,
In ethereal whispers, hearts entwine.

A canvas painted with soft dew,
Each droplet glimmers, fresh and new.
In stillness thrives a sacred trust,
In quiet moments, life is just.

With every breath, the shadows fade,
In twilight's arms, no longer strayed.
The air a symphony so pure,
In this hush, our souls endure.

The whispers fade to gentle sighs,
As dawn unfolds with blushing skies.
Yet in our hearts, that hush will stay,
A timeless echo of the day.

Crisp Overture

The morning breaks with fiery hue,
In crisp air, dreams begin anew.
Each note of dawn, a sweet refrain,
As daylight wipes the night away.

With every step on dew-kissed grass,
The world awakens, shadows pass.
A melody of rustling leaves,
A song of life that softly weaves.

The sun ascends with golden grace,
Illuminating every face.
In laughter shared and voices clear,
The overture of joy draws near.

Each moment ripe with hope and change,
As seasons shift, and worlds arrange.
In nature's chorus, we belong,
A crisp overture, a vibrant song.

So let us dance beneath the sky,
With open hearts, let laughter fly.
In every breath, the truth we find,
Crisp overture of humankind.

The Symphony of Silence

In stillness where the shadows dwell,
A symphony of silence swells.
Each note a heartbeat, deep and slow,
A tranquil ebb, a gentle flow.

The absence speaks, a voice serene,
In whispered dreams, the void between.
Where chaos fades and thoughts align,
In quiet realms, our souls entwine.

Through pauses long, through breaths we take,
A world of peace, a gentle wake.
The silence sings, a song profound,
In every inch, in every sound.

Yet in this hush, a pulse remains,
A rhythm beat in soft refrains.
The symphony of stillness grows,
A tapestry where calm bestows.

So linger here, in twilight's grace,
Embrace the still, find your own space.
In every breath, the silence thrives,
The symphony of life survives.

Frosty Dreams in Quietude

In the hush of night, dreams unfold,
A blanket of white, softly behold.
Stars whisper secrets, cold and bright,
Wrapped in the stillness, hearts take flight.

Trees adorned with shimmering ice,
Nature's artwork, pure and nice.
Silence reigns, a peaceful sound,
In frosty dreams, solace found.

Moonbeams dance on a pristine sheet,
A world transformed, oh so sweet.
Every breath, a foggy sigh,
In quietude, the spirit flies.

Footsteps muffled on snow's embrace,
Each crunch a step in a timeless space.
Wandering softly through the night,
In frosty dreams, we find the light.

Frosted Echoes

Echoes of winter, soft and low,
Through frosted branches, whispers flow.
The world is hushed, a gentle sigh,
In crystal realms where spirits lie.

Frozen ponds, reflections clear,
Nature's canvas, drawing near.
Chill in the air, a tender taste,
In quiet moments, there's no haste.

Footprints linger on the snowy ground,
Each echo telling tales profound.
In the cold glow of twilight's hue,
Frosted echoes call, anew.

A song of silence, warmly spun,
Under the watch of the faint sun.
Through frosted whispers, dreams entwine,
Echoes of winter, forever divine.

Silent Crystals

Silent crystals, glimmering bright,
Adorning the world in frosty light.
Each flake a wonder, unique and true,
Patterned beauty, in shades of blue.

Whispers of wonder fill the air,
Nature's jewels, beyond compare.
In the stillness, magic flows,
In silent crystals, the heart knows.

Frost-kissed leaves, a gentle touch,
In winter's hands, we cherish much.
Every sparkle, a fleeting chance,
Silent crystals, a winter's dance.

The world transformed, a gleaming sight,
Wrapped in the arms of the cold, white night.
Silent crystals, at twilight's end,
In their beauty, we find a friend.

Whispers of the Cold

Whispers of the cold, they sigh,
In the frosty air, where dreams fly.
A lullaby of winter's grace,
Echoes softly, time and space.

Through drifting snow, a gentle hush,
Nature pauses in twilight's blush.
Whispers linger on the breeze,
With every flake, our worries ease.

Silhouetted trees stand tall and brave,
Guardians of secrets they save.
In frosty realms, the heart takes hold,
Heeding softly the whispers of cold.

A tapestry of white, so pure,
In hidden stories, we find allure.
Each breath a cloud in the moon's sweet glow,
Guided by whispers, in the shimmering snow.

Frost-kissed Lyrics of Solitude

In a world wrapped in white,
Silent whispers take flight.
Brittle branches bend low,
Underneath the soft glow.

Footsteps crunch in the night,
Echoes of pure delight.
A blanket of peace spreads,
Where every heart treads.

Muffled sounds gently fade,
In the glistening glade.
Chill air breaths like a sigh,
In shadows, dreams lie.

Stars peek through the haze,
Illuminating dark bays.
In solitude, I find grace,
In this quiet embrace.

Frost-kissed horizons gleam,
Dancing in winter's dream.
Each moment, a soft song,
In solitude, I belong.

Hoarfrost Dreams

Morning mist drapes the ground,
In silence, beauty is found.
Hoarfrost on the leaves glistens,
Nature quietly listens.

Whispers of wintery lore,
Calling from distant shore.
Each crystal tells a tale,
Of fragile dreams that sail.

Branches wear silver crowns,
As twilight softly drowns.
In the realm of the cold,
Magic and stillness unfold.

Frosty fingers reach wide,
On this wintry glide.
In echoes of night's breath,
Is the promise of death.

Yet new life will arise,
Under pastel skies.
In hoarfrost dreams we believe,
In the wonder we weave.

The Quiet Lullaby of Snowfall

Softly whispers the snow,
As winter winds gently blow.
Each flake a quiet grace,
Falling in its own space.

Candlelight flickers near,
Drawing loved ones close here.
With blankets piled high,
We watch the night sky.

Trees stand in their white robes,
Shrouded in soft globes.
The world, hushed and serene,
Wraps us in its dream.

A lullaby for the heart,
Where warm and cold do part.
In this snowy embrace,
Find peace in the still place.

As the hours drift by,
Underneath the deep sky.
The quiet lullaby calls,
In the stillness that falls.

The Fading Voices of December

Whispers linger in air,
Fading echoes everywhere.
December's voice grows faint,
In shadows, dreams paint.

Like leaves that fall from trees,
Carried by the icy breeze.
Time slips through our hands,
A quiet, gentle strand.

Fireside tales now told,
In warmth, the hearts unfold.
Memories wrapped in light,
As stars fill the night.

The old year bids goodbye,
While new hopes start to fly.
In the silence so clear,
We hold what's precious near.

The fading voices trace,
In every loving space.
December, sweet and bold,
Leaves stories yet untold.

Glacial Serenade

Whispers in the icy breeze,
Floating dreams on chilly seas.
A crystal symphony does play,
Through glistening morn of frosty gray.

Eagles soar on frozen high,
As silver clouds drift through the sky.
The tranquil night, a cloak of light,
Enfolds the world in sleep so bright.

Mountains stand with icy grace,
Time itself in this cold place.
Each flake falls in soft embrace,
Nature's quiet, sacred space.

Stars twinkle like diamonds rare,
In the icy evening's air.
The universe sings a tune,
While the world sleeps under moon.

With every breath, the cold ignites,
A ballet of serene delights.
In each heart, the stillness stays,
In winter's dance, we find our ways.

Mirth of Ice Agaze

Laughter rings through frigid air,
Joyful hearts without a care.
Children play on frozen lakes,
As the world in winter wakes.

Snowflakes swirl like tiny sprites,
Dancing through the starry nights.
The moon's soft glow on icy ground,
In this mirth, peace is found.

Frosty whispers tease the trees,
Swaying gently with the breeze.
Nature's song in cold delight,
Brings warmth to the chilling night.

Through the fields, the shadows glide,
In their elegance, they bide.
Every pathway, bright and bold,
Tales of winter to be told.

In the hush, hear laughter rise,
An echo in the starlit skies.
This mirth, a gift so grand,
Taken by the frost's soft hand.

Flight of Frost

Across the field, the breezes play,
Wings of frost in a swift ballet.
Each breath a whisper, soft and light,
In the dance of day and night.

Icy tendrils stretch and twine,
In the air, a twinkling shine.
With each flutter, they ignite,
A cascade of shimmering white.

Clouds of snow like feathers fall,
Painting silence, calming all.
Through the air, like dreams they glide,
In this magical snowy ride.

Time stands still in this frosted land,
Where beauty dwells, soft and grand.
In the stillness, hearts take flight,
In the embrace of winter's night.

A moment captured, pure and bright,
In the embrace of tender light.
Here, the spirit finds its peace,
In the flight of frost, joys increase.

Bated Breath of Silence

Within the woods, a stillness grows,
Wrapped in winter's silent shows.
Each whisper lost in crystal air,
Breath held tight in nature's care.

Branches wear their coats of lace,
Softly veiling every place.
In the hush, the world abides,
With secrets where the silence hides.

Footsteps soft on powdered ground,
Quiet echoes all around.
Every sound, a fleeting ghost,
In this peace, we cherish most.

Frosted nature's quiet hymn,
Starlit skies, the edges dim.
In bated breath, we come to feel,
The stillness, oh, so surreal.

As night unfolds its velvet cloak,
In the silence, hearts invoke.
Moments linger, time unwinds,
In this stillness, peace we find.

Echoes of Crystal Dreams

In night's embrace, stars softly gleam,
Memories linger, as shadows teem.
Whispers of wishes, lost in the mist,
The heart's soft longing, too sweet to resist.

Echoes of laughter, like tinkling bells,
Through corridors of dreams, where silence dwells.
In crystal caverns, reflections dance,
Revealing the secrets of fate and chance.

Moonlight cascades on a silver stream,
Carrying stories that float like a dream.
Each ripple tells tales of forgotten lore,
Unlocking the whispers that time can restore.

In the quiet moments, truth unfolds clear,
Voices of the past are all that we hear.
Drifting through the fabric of night so deep,
In echoes of crystal, we find what we keep.

A tapestry woven with love and despair,
In dreams we wander, beyond all compare.
Through echoes of time, we forever chase,
The beauty of moments, a fleeting embrace.

Frost's Soft Serenade

Morning breaks with a gentle hush,
Frost blankets fields in a silvery rush.
Nature holds its breath in the cold, still air,
As winter whispers secrets, tender and rare.

Tree branches shimmer with gleaming frost,
Each crystal formed, a moment embossed.
Sunlight dances, igniting a glow,
In frost's soft serenade, life starts to flow.

Footsteps crunch on a carpet of white,
The world painted fresh, pure and bright.
Each breath is visible, a fleeting sigh,
In this hushed realm, the spirit can fly.

Chill bites the cheeks, a refreshing embrace,
While the heart finds warmth in this tranquil space.
Nature's lullaby, a sweet, mellow tone,
In frost's soft serenade, we're never alone.

As the day fades, colors start to blend,
Evening's arrival, a warm, soft friend.
Under a blanket of stars, dreams cascade,
In the hush of the night, we find love displayed.

Whispering Pines in White

In the forest deep, where silence reigns,
Whispering pines wear their winter chains.
Clad in pure white, they stand tall and grand,
Guardians of secrets in this frozen land.

Snowflakes drift down, a delicate dance,
In the heart of the woods, a fleeting chance.
Each branch bows low with the weight of the snow,
Whispers of nature in a hushed undertow.

Echoes of wind through the needles ring,
Soft melodies, the winter's sweet offering.
Time seems to pause, as the world comes alive,
In whispering pines, our spirits will thrive.

Footprints in snow mark the path we take,
In the stillness of wonder, our hearts awake.
Every rustling pine tells a tale of old,
In whispers of wisdom, their stories unfold.

As twilight descends and shadows embrace,
Moonlight casts silver, transforming the space.
In the hush of the night, with the cold air in sight,
Whispering pines guard our dreams and delight.

Gleaming Silence

In the still of the night, all is at rest,
Gleaming silence, nature's gentle best.
Stars twinkle bright in the velvet sky,
As whispers of dreams begin to fly.

Softly the moon spills its silvery light,
Casting shadows that dance in the night.
Each rustle and sigh holds a story untold,
In the heart of the silence, treasures unfold.

The world pauses here, in a moment so pure,
In gleaming silence, our souls find the cure.
With every heartbeat, we feel the embrace,
Of quiet communion in this sacred space.

Voices of stillness, though soft, resonate,
In the calm of the night, we await fate.
In glimmers of hope, all worries take flight,
Gleaming silence sings of eternal delight.

As dawn's early light begins to break through,
Colors awaken, painting a new view.
In the symphony of night, we find our refrain,
In gleaming silence, our hearts beat again.

Melodies Beneath the Snow

In silence lie the whispers, soft,
Where flakes of white in dance aloft,
They cradle dreams of warmth untold,
Beneath the blanket, secrets old.

The earth is hushed, a gentle sigh,
As winter's hand draws nigh the sky,
Each crystal note a fleeting prayer,
For spring's embrace, a love affair.

With every flake that settles near,
A lullaby for all to hear,
In frosted air, the echoes play,
Of summertime so far away.

Yet here we find a quiet peace,
In every drift, a sweet release,
The world transformed in white's embrace,
Melodies of grace we trace.

So let the hush entwine our hearts,
Melodies soft as winter departs,
In fleeting time, we come to see,
The beauty of what's meant to be.

Tones of the Frozen Breeze

A breath of chill upon the skin,
The frozen breeze, a subtle din,
It whispers soft through bough and pine,
With nature's song, a soft design.

The icicles play their crystal chime,
Each drop of water sings in rhyme,
The harmony of cold and light,
In every gust, the world feels right.

Each swirling flake, a note reborn,
In fleeting flight, the air adorned,
They spiral down, a dance so free,
Twisting through the frosty spree.

In this embrace of winter's grace,
We find our warmth in nature's face,
The tones of cold, a sweet refrain,
Inviting us to dance again.

So let us wander through the chill,
With every gust, our spirits thrill,
For in the tones that blend and weave,
We find the joy that we believe.

Harmony in Hibernation

In slumber deep, the world lies still,
With dreams that gleam and hearts to fill,
The earth, a canvas painted white,
In peace obscured from day to night.

The creatures nest in cozy warmth,
In hidden dens, away from harm,
They dream of spring, of blooms renewed,
In restful pause, their lives pursued.

The silence sings of hope and care,
As winter weaves its magic rare,
Each breath a promise yet to bloom,
Within the quiet, hearts consume.

So let us dwell in calm embrace,
Finding peace in winter's grace,
For in this time of soft retreat,
We sow our dreams and find our beat.

And when the thaw begins to sing,
Awakening, we'll take to wing,
In harmony, we greet the day,
Rejoicing in life's grand ballet.

The Stillness of Ice

Beneath the glassy surface wide,
The world is still, as if to bide,
A moment paused in time's embrace,
The frozen stillness fills the space.

With every crack, a tale concealed,
Of whispers shared, of hearts revealed,
The dance of light on surfaces rare,
From shadows cast, the secrets bare.

The chilly breath of winter's kiss,
Creates a world of tranquil bliss,
In frozen realms where dreams reside,
The beauty found in calm and pride.

Each flurry boasts a tale untold,
In frozen frames, memories hold,
So let us pause and take it in,
The stillness of where life begins.

As seasons shift and melt away,
The memories in ice will stay,
For in this quiet, we shall see,
The echoes of what used to be.

Glistening Apprehensions

In shadows cast by whispering trees,
A silver moon hangs softly in the breeze.
Fleeting thoughts like moths in flight,
Dance around the edge of night.

With every glimmer, doubts reside,
Caught in the web where fears abide.
Yet in the dark, a spark will grow,
Illuminating what we know.

Through fragile hearts, a longing stirs,
The silent pulse of hopes deferred.
But even in the darkest place,
Dreams can find a tender space.

So we grasp the moments near,
Each glint a guide to face our fear.
With every breath, the journey starts,
Revealing strength within our hearts.

Beneath the stars, we rise and shine,
Embracing life, both yours and mine.
In glistening apprehensions laid,
We find the courage we have made.

Winter's Gentle Embrace

Softly falls the gentle snow,
A blanket white, where silence grows.
Each flake a whisper from above,
Wrapping the world in warmth and love.

The trees, adorned with crystal lace,
Stand tall and still in winter's grace.
While hearths burn bright with flickering light,
A refuge found through cold, long night.

Footprints trace the hidden paths,
As laughter echoes, the cold just laughs.
Children play in frosty air,
Each moment cherished, pure and rare.

The warmth of cocoa, sweet and spiced,
Spills joy in cups, each sip enticed.
And as the twilight softly sighs,
The stars begin to fill the skies.

In winter's hold, we find our peace,
An inner warmth that will not cease.
For in the stillness, love remains,
In winter's gentle, soft refrains.

Melodic Reflections in Still Air

In stillness wide, the echoes sing,
A tune from far, of endless spring.
The gentle sway of time at play,
Turns silence into a soft ballet.

Reflections dance upon the stream,
Each ripple holds a fleeting dream.
As whispers weave through ancient pines,
A melody of timeless lines.

The softest breeze carries the notes,
Of stories told by passing boats.
In twilight's grasp, the world feels small,
Yet holds the beauty of it all.

Through fragrant blooms and rustling leaves,
We find the warmth that nature weaves.
The moments stretch in twilight's hue,
Melodic reflections, pure and true.

Beneath the veil of starry skies,
We breathe the song that never dies.
In stillness found, we learn to care,
With melodic reflections in still air.

Chill's Caress at Nightfall

As shadows fall and daylight fades,
The world is draped in twilight's shades.
A chill invades the evening's calm,
A haunting touch, a whispered balm.

The echo of the day's retreat,
Brings whispered secrets to the street.
Beneath the stars, the cold will creep,
Into our hearts while others sleep.

Each breath released in frosty air,
A fleeting glimpse, a gentle stare.
As darkness blankets all around,
In silence deep, our thoughts resound.

The moon, a lantern in the night,
Glistens softly, a guiding light.
With chill's embrace, we find a place,
To pause, reflect, and feel the grace.

And though the night is cold and deep,
We cherish warmth in dreams we keep.
In every chill, there lies a call,
To rise and shine, embracing all.

Cadences Beneath Thick Blankets

Soft whispers ride the evening breeze,
Underneath the thick blankets, we freeze.
Hushed tones echo through the silent night,
In dreams, we wander, hearts taking flight.

The world outside, a canvas pure and wide,
As we cocoon in warmth, side by side.
Gentle rhythms, a lullaby's call,
Embraced in stillness, we savor it all.

Each heartbeat resonates, a sacred sound,
In the quietude where love is found.
Wrapped in layers, both tender and true,
The night dances softly, just me and you.

Snowflakes fall like confetti from the sky,
Painting our memories, as time slips by.
Cadences of winter, tender and light,
We find our harmony beneath the night.

Under thick blankets, the world fades away,
In this intimate haven, forever we'll stay.
The cadence of love, a sweet serenade,
In the warmth of our hearts, fears gently laid.

The Dance of Winter's Veil

Beneath the pale moon, the world drifts slow,
In winter's embrace, our souls start to glow.
A dance of white flakes, they twirl and spin,
Casting a magic that flows from within.

Branches adorned in a frosted attire,
Whispers of snowflakes, the air, they inspire.
Footsteps trace patterns on carpets of white,
As shadows and whispers converge into night.

Each breath turns to mist, a soft lullaby,
In the stillness we hear the night's gentle sigh.
The dance of winter weaves tales from afar,
Unfolding the secrets hidden in stars.

A flicker of warmth amidst chill's sharp embrace,
In the heart of the winter, we find our place.
In twirls and in glides, the snow speaks our name,
In the dance of winter, we'll never be the same.

As each flake falls, weaving dreams on the ground,
In the dance of winter, our spirits are found.
Together we twirl in this frozen ballet,
Underneath the stars, we glide far away.

Whispers in the Snowdrifts

Whispers float gently on the brisk air,
Each snowdrift cradles secrets to share.
In the hush of the night, a promise is made,
Memories woven, in frost we cascade.

Footsteps are muffled, the world lies still,
In the silence, our hearts know this thrill.
A blanket of snow, soft as a sigh,
Encircling our dreams, where the lost hopes lie.

Each flake tells a story, unique and bright,
In the canvas of white, our spirits ignite.
We listen to echoes of whispers that fade,
In the warmth of the night, our fears are allayed.

Underneath the stars, we lean close and breathe,
In the chill of the air, our spirits believe.
Dancing through snowdrifts, we twirl and we spin,
In whispers of winter, true love will begin.

With fingers entwined, in the soft, quiet glow,
In whispers of snowdrifts, affection will grow.
The world fades away, just our hearts and the stars,
In the intimate night, we find who we are.

Crystal Carols under the Stars

Under starlit heavens, the night comes alive,
Crystal carols echo, in dreams we thrive.
The world wrapped in silver, glistens and glows,
A wonderland whispered, where magic flows.

Notes dance on the air, a melody sweet,
In the heart of the night where the dreamers meet.
The chorus of winter sings clear and bright,
As joy fills the silence, embracing the night.

Stars twinkle like diamonds, adorning the dome,
Together we wander, far away from home.
In the chill, we find warmth, wrapped in delight,
With crystal carols, our hearts take flight.

Each breath forms a puff in the frosty air,
With you by my side, there's nothing to spare.
The joy of the season glimmers in our eyes,
In crystal carols whispered beneath the skies.

So let the night linger, let the music play,
In this snowy embrace, we'll forever stay.
With each note that rises, our souls will unite,
Crystal carols ringing, in the heart of the night.

Melodies in the Muffled Air

Soft whispers twirl in the night,
Carried gently from sight.
Stars blink in silent cheer,
While echoes drift near.

Melodies in the Muffled Air

Moonlight weaves through the trees,
Playing tunes with the breeze.
Leaves rustle, a floating grace,
In this serene space.

Melodies in the Muffled Air

Dreams hang like silver threads,
Binding hearts, where hope spreads.
In shadows, soft sounds blend,
Whispering without end.

Melodies in the Muffled Air

A symphony of the night,
Crafted by stars so bright.
Each note drifts through the air,
A moment sweet and rare.

Melodies in the Muffled Air

Time pauses in this place,
Filling souls with its grace.
As if the world can hear,
The music we hold dear.

Melodies in the Muffled Air

With every heartbeat aligned,
Harmony gently defined.
In this moment, we share,
A song beyond compare.

Frostbitten Harmonies

Frost glistens like tiny stars,
Nature's art, no need for bars.
Each breath forms a delicate mist,
In this cold, we do exist.

Frostbitten Harmonies

Branches creak under the weight,
Whispers echo, softly great.
Icicles dangle and sway,
Nature sings in its way.

Frostbitten Harmonies

Footsteps crunch on frozen ground,
In the stillness, peace is found.
Winter's breath wraps us tight,
In the depths of long night.

Frostbitten Harmonies

Glowing embers in the fire,
Warming hearts with desire.
Together we face the chill,
In the quiet, time stands still.

Frostbitten Harmonies

Sparkling dreams in wintry embrace,
Filling the air with grace.
Every note, sharp yet bright,
Guides us through the night.

Frostbitten Harmonies

In frostbitten landscapes we roam,
Finding solace, a joyful home.
With each melody we share,
We find warmth in the air.

Crescendo of Crystalline Dreams

Glistening shards of light,
Reflecting dreams in sight.
Each moment holds a refrain,
Echoing joy and pain.

Crescendo of Crystalline Dreams

Fractured glimmers, soft and bright,
Shimmering in the cool night.
Winds carry tales untold,
In this realm, brave and bold.

Crescendo of Crystalline Dreams

With each step, a new song blooms,
Breaking free from winter's glooms.
In the silence, words take flight,
Sailing softly through the night.

Crescendo of Crystalline Dreams

Moonlight casts a silver lace,
In our hearts, we find our place.
Each note a breath of air,
Carried on currents rare.

Crescendo of Crystalline Dreams

Here we dance in frosted light,
Lost in dreams, pure delight.
A symphony born of grace,
Carving time to embrace.

Crescendo of Crystalline Dreams

With every heartbeat, we rise,
Chasing dreams beneath the skies.
In crystalline whispers, we gleam,
United in one perfect dream.

Dances of the Icy Breeze

Whirling whispers through the trees,
The world sways with the icy breeze.
Snowflakes twirl like gentle sighs,
Painting tales beneath vast skies.

Dances of the Icy Breeze

Nature's rhythm fills the air,
As branches sway in soft despair.
The chill carries secrets profound,
In every rustle, magic's found.

Dances of the Icy Breeze

Footprints meld into the white,
Paths unwound in fading light.
With every gust, we embrace,
Icy dances, a sacred space.

Dances of the Icy Breeze

Twinkling stars, a frozen choir,
Conducted by the night's desire.
The wind sings through frosty leaves,
In this ballet, our heart believes.

Dances of the Icy Breeze

Together, we glide and spin,
Lost in the magic within.
With laughter echoing so bright,
We dance in winter's light.

Dances of the Icy Breeze

In every swirl, a story told,
As the night air turns to gold.
Leaving traces in the snow,
Our spirits rise, beautifully aglow.

Milton Keynes UK
Ingram Content Group UK Ltd.
UKHW021358081224
452111UK00007B/98

9 789908 521107